Read & Respond

FOR KS2

Read & Respond

FOR KS2

Author: Celia Warren

Development Editor: Alex Albrighton

Editor: Pam Kelt

Assistant Editor: Margaret Eaton

Series Designer: Anna Oliwa

Designer: Liz Gilbert

Illustrations: Karen Donnelly

Text © 2010 Celia Warren © 2010 Scholastic Ltd

Designed using Adobe InDesign

Published by Scholastic Ltd.
Book End, Range Road, Witney,
Oxfordshire OX29 0YD
www.scholastic.co.uk

Printed by Bell & Bain

1 2 3 4 5 6 7 8 9   0 1 2 3 4 5 6 7 8 9

British Library Cataloguing-in-Publication Data
A catalogue record for this book is available from the
British Library.

ISBN 978-1407-11350-0

Acknowledgements

The publishers gratefully acknowledge permission to reproduce the following copyright material: **HarperCollins Publishers** for the use of extracts from *Private Peaceful* by Michael Morpurgo © 2003, Michael Morpurgo (2003, HarperCollins). **The Society of Authors** for the use of 'For the Fallen' by Laurence Binyon from *The Times – 21st September, 1914* © 1914, Laurence Binyon. Every effort has been made to trace copyright holders for the works reproduced in this book, and the publishers apologise for any inadvertent omissions.

Private Peaceful

About the book

Michael Morpurgo's portrayal of the era of the First World War provides the setting for a novel that is a tribute to those who fought for their country – especially to those who were executed for often spurious reasons. Shell shock was not understood at the time and young men, some still boys, too young to have enlisted, were shot at dawn, after brief courts martial, for the crimes of cowardice, desertion or falling asleep on watch. At the time of publication, in 2003, the government was still refusing a posthumous pardon to these young men, but relented three years later.

This novel is the story of three fictional brothers, one of whom is brain-damaged after suffering babyhood meningitis. The other two enlist in the army – the elder, Charlie, through pressure of blackmail at the hands of the Colonel, and the younger, Tommo, through loyalty to his brother. They share a strong love, not only for their mother and brother, but for Molly, a friend since early school days. Tommo carries a painful secret that he longs but fails to tell: he feels responsible for an accident that killed his father. When, at last, he does share his guilty secret, it is to discover that the family already knew of his anxiety – he talked in his sleep.

The story is told in alternating narrative that switches between the present day (at the Belgian front) and recollections of the narrator's life. Tommo's voice tells the story from these two perspectives. It emerges, as time ticks by, that Private Peaceful is to be executed at dawn. It is not until the end of the book that readers learn which of the brothers is to die.

Guilt, fear, bullying (formal and informal), love, loyalty, bravery, cowardice, faith, belief and forgiveness are all explored as the characters progress from innocence to experience, raising many issues for discussion. There is also the opportunity to examine social hierarchy and how the war influenced change, including treatment of the mentally handicapped.

Inspiration for the novel grew from Michael Morpurgo's visit to Ypres war cemetery, as well as his interviewing three veterans from the trenches. The name 'Private Peaceful' was borrowed from a Ypres headstone, but the character in the book is fictional. The novel has also been adapted as a play by scriptwriter Simon Reade.

Private Peaceful is a novel that tackles moving and poignant themes, and is perhaps best suited to smaller groups and children of sufficient emotional maturity.

About the author

Michael Morpurgo was born in 1943 and is married with children and grandchildren. Telling stories that held the children's interest, when he was working as a primary school teacher, made him realise that he wanted to work magic for children as an author. In 2003 he became Children's Laureate for two years, a post which he and Poet Laureate Ted Hughes had inaugurated a few years earlier.

In 1976, with the help of his wife, Clare, Michael Morpurgo founded a charity called Farms for City Children, where children living in a city, with no knowledge of the countryside, have the opportunity to stay for a week and experience life on a working farm.

Facts and figures

Private Peaceful is Michael Morpurgo's 100th book and has gone on to win several awards, including the Blue Peter Book Award 2005 in the UK, the Red House Book Award in 2004, and the California Young Reader Medal in the Young Adult category for 2007–2008.

Other Morpurgo books on the theme of the First World War include *The Best Christmas Present in the World* and *War Horse*.

Guided reading

Before reading

A photocopiable glossary on page 22 of this book explains terms relating specifically to the First World War. Other unfamiliar words could be added to a class glossary. *Private Peaceful* deals with distressing events and it may help sensitive children to view the work as a respectful tribute to those who died unnecessarily or unfairly. (You could compare it with Tennyson's *The Charge of the Light Brigade* about the blundering command in the Crimean war.)

Five past ten

Ensure that the children realise that, in the opening narrative of this and every chapter, the narrator is aged nearly 18. Accounts following the butterfly logo are of times gone by in the same narrator's life, a retrospective of his childhood, in whatever tense they are written. Point out there is no indication of who *They* (*have gone now*) refers to.

Discuss Tommo's statement that Charlie has *done everything and knows everything*. Ask: *How accurate is that description? Why might a younger brother think that?* Draw attention to the changes to present tense, making Tommo's memories particularly graphic. Explain *commandments*, akin to, and overlapping with, the biblical ten Commandments from God. Create a glossary of unfamiliar words: *mesmerised* (enthralled, entranced), *tribulation* (ordeal, suffering), *belfry* (bell space in church tower) and *pulpit* (raised, roofed platform for preachers). Explain *touch our forelocks* (in imitation of removing a hat, showing deference to superiors).

Twenty to eleven

Talk about the passage of present time between chapters (here, 35 minutes). Invite the children to discuss occasions and circumstances that put people off eating: nervousness, excitement, anticipation, fear, distress or grief.

Explain the seriousness of meningitis, an infection of the brain which, without antibiotics, can cause brain damage or even death. After Jimmy Parsons' name-calling and the ensuing fight, invite the children to compare how the bully takes his punishment with how Charlie does. Discuss why Jimmy's repeated *Ow, sir!* sounds comical – at once less brave than the silent Charlie, and deferential to the Head.

Talk about the Colonel's use of blackmail to force Tommo's mother to work for him. Ask: *Why does Tommo observe that the Colonel 'could not help but hear us'?* How does that make him feel better? (It demonstrates that he can't break their family spirit.)

Nearly quarter past eleven

Discuss how the mouse in Tommo's present-time experience triggers his memories of mice: each episode points to attitudes of the main characters. Draw attention to Molly's religious rhetoric at the mouse's funeral, how she knows the 'language' of a strict, puritanical, narrow-minded form of religion, screaming at Grandma Wolf that she will *go to Hell*. Explore why the Colonel's wife's death is described as *a miracle*. Ask: *Why?* (Relief at Mother's return and Grandma Wolf's departure.) Discuss how Molly's ceremony with the stones resembles religious ritual, and how Tommo's recognition that he and Charlie never say their prayers any more, Big Joe's singing of 'Oranges and Lemons', and the boys' crossed fingers, all help to reduce religion to superstition.

Ten to midnight

This chapter begins with Tommo's affirmation of the decline of his religious faith. Draw attention to the significance and impact of Tommo's falling asleep. Compare this with his determination to stay awake throughout this night of looking back.

Grandma Wolf's shame of her relations echoes that mentioned at Father's funeral, when Tommo says, *I didn't really understand why until later, until I was older*. As Grandma Wolf becomes 'Wolfwoman', Tommo learns of her relationship with the Colonel, explaining her low opinion of her family. Explain *hiding* (a beating).

Point out how the children's growing up, and growing apart, is portrayed through repeated use of the first-person pronoun in Tommo's account: *I think* and so on. Talk about how Charlie's return from work reinforces his adulthood, behaving as Father had.

Point out how the author forces comparison of the worry or horror of situations by lining them up side by side: Tommo's hatred of Mr Munnings in the aftermath of his bullying, and the implications of Charlie having stolen the Colonel's dog.

Twenty-four minutes past twelve

Discuss why the titles grow more precise with each chapter. (It imitates the narrator's increasing awareness of every precious minute, fending off morning.)

Encourage the children to examine how snippets of information reflect the era: Molly reading the Colonel's newspaper (with the throwaway irony *so she knew it had to be true*) while ironing it, Mother *setting her sewing aside* (working, even at home), and how such details present a stark contrast to the war's onset, and its distant causes. Invite possible answers to Molly's chapter-closing rhetorical question.

Add to the glossary: *despicable* (shameful, disgraceful); *dumbfounded* (lost for words); *in his seventh heaven* (utterly contented); *breathing down his neck* (watching him closely); *gesticulating* (making gestures to point or explain, without words); *rendezvous* (pronounced ron-day-voo) meetings; and *supercilious* (scornfully superior).

Nearly five to one

Point out how much conversation is reported speech rather than direct, such as *We didn't have any choice, she said…* Ask: *How does this affect the pace of storytelling?* Invite the children to compare Mother's inability to drink tea when Big Joe is missing with Tommo's earlier lack of appetite as he reminisces. Identify the emotions that made

Tommo cry and sing simultaneously. (Relief and joy.) After reading Big Joe's first direct speech, ask: *How might his style of speech have been misconstrued if used earlier in the story? How does it sound once we know Big Joe's background?* (Poignant rather than humorous.) Add to the glossary: *scenario* (situation, state of affairs) and *parapet* (low wall).

Twenty-eight minutes past one

Discuss how common causes (like searching for Big Joe) bring communities together. Explain *bad blood* (deep, long-held grudges). Draw attention to how Charlie's initial, measured response to Molly's news emulates and prolongs the tension as the family await his reaction. Alert the children to the fact that, again, the Colonel uses blackmail as a bullying tactic, forcing Charlie to enlist. Discuss why Tommo compares his two years' soldiering to being in a tunnel, and *a lifetime*.

Explain the historic slang term *tickety-boo* (fine, brilliant) and, conversely, *no picnic*; also, *to wet the baby's head* (have a drink to celebrate the baby's birth, echoing the literal wetting of a baby's head at Christian baptism) and *parrying* (warding off, dodging).

Fourteen minutes past two

This chapter introduces formal bullying in army training. Check that the children understand the term *jumping through hoops* – degrading, unquestioning obedience. Can they think of any value to soldiers responding like trained, performing animals? (Instinctive responses might save lives?) Add to the glossary *cheek by jowl* (close together) and *a bit of a Jonah* (someone who is a channel for disaster to strike).

Draw attention to the analogy of actors at a rehearsal, suggesting how the boys' situation seems unreal. Invite the children to compare Hanley's bullying with that of Munnings and the Colonel. Discuss how, if at all, this is worse. Explain the phrase *broken ranks* (stepped out of line without permission).

Guided reading

A minute past three

Look at why the author chooses 'Oranges and Lemons' as Big Joe's favourite song, comparing the last two lines and the childish innocence of the earlier lines about London church bells. Discuss the irony of the soldiers' relief at reaching the front. Ask: *What does their use of a nickname reveal about Captain Wilkes?* Clarify the pronunciation of French words: *château* (shat-oh) and *estaminet* (ess-tam-in-ay). Add the word *meticulous* to the class glossary (careful, precise). Explain how a lit cigarette tip acts like a target flare in the dark, inviting accurate enemy fire. Encourage the children to notice the tense effect of short sentences such as *Then he does.*

Twenty-five past three

Again there is no indication who *They* are, except for the padre. Point out how one adjective (*vanishing*) indicates the mouse's departure. Clarify the ownership of the field-grey (German) and khaki (British) uniforms. Can the children guess what the *sickly-sweet stench* that *no-one dared speak of* was? (Blood.) Can they explain the significance of the italicised *Y'aint a coward, are you?* followed by Tommo's internal response? Add to the glossary *pipsqueak* (unimportant person) and *wangle* (secure desired result by devious means). Ask: *Does 'wangle' seem appropriate, considering Charlie's injury? What does use of this verb say about Charlie?*

Nearly four o'clock

Discuss how information is divulged drip by drip in the present narrative with nothing spelled out

and readers left to speculate 'who' and 'how'. Draw attention to *old soldiers* referring to experience, not age.

Ask: *Why is there no sense of rejoicing when Tommo learns that Jimmy Parsons, his old tormenter, has been killed?* Discuss the meaning of *Sunday-school Heaven* and *Big Joe's happy Heaven.*

Five to five

Draw attention to Tommo's rhetorical questions that invite no answers. The reader now knows for sure it will be death by firing squad at dawn and the person will be a Private Peaceful. Ask: *Will it be Charlie or Tommo?* (Remind the children of Charlie's signature on his letter, *the other Private Peaceful.) Does Sergeant Hanley's comment make it clearer later in this chapter?*

Together with the children, identify the sequence of sense-awareness as Tommo describes waking, half-buried and injured, but alive (in present tense): sound, (lack of) sight, touch, sound again, sight.

Add to the class glossary the phrase *cooked my goose* (in irrevocable trouble; done for). Can the children infer the meaning of *My silence was enough*?

One minute to six

Point out that it is only in this last chapter that we learn that Tommo is in a hay barn. Ask: *Which parts (if any) of Tommo's description of Charlie's execution does he witness, rather than imagine?* (Rifle volley.)

Discuss the closing sentences: an 'open ending', for the reader to decide whether or not Tommo will survive.

Shared reading

Extract 1

- Explain that in the first chapter, the author introduces all the main characters. Four appear in this extract, which is the opening of the retrospective narrative as Tommo recalls his life, beginning here with his first day at school.
- Underline words in the first paragraph that strongly indicate Tommo's physical and emotional discomfort: *choking, strange, heavy, dread, terrible, raging* and *whipping*.
- In the second paragraph, invite the children to compare descriptions that relate to Big Joe's life at home, underlining: *singing, laughing, happy*.
- Circle and count each use of the first person pronoun, *I*. Read aloud the sentiments that follow: *I don't want, I dread, I wish* and so on. Talk about how this helps the reader to identify with the child's first journey to school; his every thought and feeling.
- Highlight the one piece of direct speech. Discuss what can be read into that one word, *Piggyback?* Talk about its effect on the little boy and what it indicates about Charlie.

Extract 2

- Underline metaphorical phrases: *beat about the bush, no picnic, on your doorstep, swallowed her up in one gulp, taken a... slice, beat them at their own game, knock the stuffing out of them*. Invite the children to infer the meaning of these phrases from the context.
- Add unfamiliar words and phrases to a class glossary: *tickety-boo* (fine; perfect) and *Hun* (derogatory word for Germans).
- Circle the word *Only* in the first paragraph, explaining this is an incomplete sentence, taking the opening *There is (only one question...)* as understood.
- Underline short sentences that speed up the speech to sound like an onslaught of gunfire – sharp, repeated, attacking, provocative.
- Explain that, although the characters are fictional, the settings are real. Hatherleigh is a market town in Devon, typical of small, close-knit communities all over Britain.
- Circle the verbs *raked (His eyes raked over us)* and *roared ("Yes!" we roared in unison)*. Invite suggestions as to how these two strong verbs are linked in terms of cause and effect, as is the use of dramatic metaphor, already underlined, in the sergeant major's choice of words.

Extract 3

- Highlight use of the adverbs *clumsily, feverishly, frantically*, descriptively prolonging the effect of the time it takes for the soldiers to react to the gas attack.
- Circle the first-person pronouns: *I, We, us, our, me, my*, pointing out how they, combined with the present tense, add immediacy to the event.
- Underline each verb used in the present participle: *rolling, searching, scenting, wafting, swallowing, snaking, stinging, burning* (relating to the gas); *praying, running, staggering, falling, shouting, grabbing, knocking, coughing, retching, choking* (relating to soldiers). Point out how this emphasises the lengthy continuation of events.
- Highlight examples of the author's use of aggressive personification of the gas – *scenting me, searching for me; swallowing everything in its path; wants... to kill us all*.
- Circle examples of alliteration and assonance that help the prose to flow as smoothly as the gas (*killer cloud, deadly tendrils... ahead, feeling... forward, wafting... wire... swallowing*).

Extract 1

Five past ten

Charlie is taking me by the hand, leading me because he knows I don't want to go. I've never worn a collar before and it's choking me. My boots are strange and heavy on my feet. My heart is heavy too, because I dread what I am going to. Charlie has told me often how terrible this school-place is: about Mr Munnings and his raging tempers and the long whipping cane he hangs on the wall above his desk.

Big Joe doesn't have to go to school and I don't think that's fair at all. He's much older than me. He's even older than Charlie and he's never been to school. He stays at home with Mother, and sits up in his tree singing *Oranges and Lemons*, and laughing. Big Joe is always happy, always laughing. I wish I could be happy like him. I wish I could be at home like him. I don't want to go with Charlie. I don't want to go to school.

I look back, over my shoulder, hoping for a reprieve, hoping that Mother will come running after me and take me home. But she doesn't come and she doesn't come, and school and Mr Munnings and his cane are getting closer with every step.

"Piggyback?" says Charlie. He sees my eyes full of tears and knows how it is. Charlie always knows how it is. He's three years older than me, so he's done everything and knows everything. He's strong, too, and very good at piggybacks. So I hop up and cling on tight, crying behind my closed eyes, trying not to whimper out loud. But I cannot hold back my sobbing for long because I know that this morning is not the beginning of anything – not new and exciting as Mother says it is – but rather the end of my beginning.

Text © 2003, Michael Morpurgo; illustration © 2010, Karen Donnelly.

Extract 2

Twenty-eight minutes past one

"I shan't beat about the bush, ladies and gentlemen," he began. "I shan't tell you it's all tickety-boo out there in France – there's been too much of that nonsense already in my view. I've been there. I've seen it for myself. So I'll tell you straight. It's no picnic. It's hard slog, that's what it is, hard slog. Only one question to ask yourself about this war. Who would you rather see marching through your streets? Us lot or the Hun? Make up your minds. Because, mark my words, ladies and gentlemen, if we don't stop them out in France the Germans will be here, right here in Hatherleigh, right here on your doorstep."

I could feel the silence all around.

"They'll come marching through here burning your houses, killing your children, and yes, violating your women. They've beaten brave little Belgium, swallowed her up in one gulp. And now they've taken a fair slice of France too. I'm here to tell you that unless we beat them at their own game, they'll gobble us up as well." His eyes raked over us. "Well? Do you want the Hun here? Do you?"

"No!" came the shout, and I was shouting along with them.

"Shall we knock the stuffing out of them then?"

"Yes!" we roared in unison.

The sergeant major nodded. "Good. Very good. Then we shall need you." He was pointing his stick now into the crowd, picking out the men, "You, and you and you." He was looking straight at me now, into my eyes. "And you too, my lad!"

Until that very moment it had honestly never occurred to me that what he was saying had anything to do with me. I had been an onlooker. No longer.

"Your king needs you. Your country needs you. And all the brave lads out in France need you too."

Text © 2003, Michael Morpurgo; illustration © 2010, Karen Donnelly

Extract 3

Nearly four o'clock

"Gas! Gas!"

The cry goes up and is echoed all along the trench. For a moment we are frozen with panic. We have trained for this time and again, but nonetheless we fumble clumsily, feverishly with our gas masks.

"Fix bayonets!" Hanley's yelling while we're still trying frantically to pull on our gas masks. We grab our rifles and fix bayonets. We're on the firestep looking out into no-man's-land, and we see it rolling towards us, this dreaded killer cloud we have heard so much about but have never seen for ourselves until now. Its deadly tendrils are searching ahead, feeling their way forward in long yellow wisps, scenting me, searching for me. Then finding me out, the gas turns and drifts straight for me. I'm shouting inside my gas mask. "Christ! Christ!" Still the gas comes on, wafting over our wire, through our wire, swallowing everything in its path...

...The gas is only feet away now. In a moment it will be on me, around me, in me. I crouch down hiding my face between my knees, hands over my helmet, praying it will float over my head, over the top of the trench and seek out someone else. But it does not. It's all around me. I tell myself I will not breathe, I must not breathe. Through a yellow mist I see the trench filling up with it. It drifts into the dugouts, snaking into every nook and cranny, looking for me. It wants to seek us all out, to kill us all, every one of us. Still I do not breathe. I see men running, staggering, falling. I hear Pete shouting out for me. Then he's grabbing me and we run. I have to breathe now. I can't run without breathing. Half-blinded by my mask I trip and fall, crashing my head against the trench wall, knocking myself half-senseless. My gas mask has come off. I pull it down, but I have breathed in and know already it's too late. My eyes are stinging. My lungs are burning. I am coughing, retching, choking.

Text © 2003, Michael Morpurgo; illustration © 2010, Karen Donnelly.

Plot, character and setting

Introductions

> **Objective:** To understand underlying themes, causes and points of view.
> **What you need:** Copies of *Private Peaceful*, enlarged copy of Extract 1 (page 8) and highlighter pens.

What to do

● Read aloud the book's three opening paragraphs, explaining that Tommo is the first-person narrator. Ask: *Do we know who They are? Do we need to know yet?*
● Ask what the children can tell about the character as implied in the opening paragraphs: *How old is he? What mood is he in?* (Reflective, desperate, determined.)
● Discuss why the narrator refers to his life so far as *yesterdays* and *tomorrows*? (*Yesterdays*, good or bad, are safely in the past; *tomorrows* hold uncertainty, or threat.)
● Explain the textual structure: the butterfly logo separating present and past. Discuss the choice of logo. Ask: *What do you associate with butterflies?* (Peace, summer, gentleness, freedom to fly, fragility.)
● Display an enlarged copy of Extract 1 on page 8. Read and annotate the text (see notes on page 7).
● Ask: *How does the repetition of she doesn't come... reflect the boy's expectations?*
● Talk about how, though looking solely through the young child's eyes, we can learn about Charlie and Mother. Ask: *What does Charlie's behaviour, and single-word question, reveal about the brothers' relationship? How, and in what light, has Mother prepared Tommo for school?*

> **Differentiation**
> **For older/more confident learners:** Ask the children to read to the end of the first chapter, discussing with a partner the events and Tommo's feelings.
> **For younger/less confident learners:** Read the first chapter with a small group, asking questions at intervals such as: *Why can't Tommo tell anyone of his feelings of guilt about Father's death?*

Character clues

> **Objective:** To infer writer's perspective from what is written and from what is implied.
> **What you need:** Copies of *Private Peaceful*, copies of photocopiable page 15 and writing materials.

What to do

● Ask the children, when they finish the second chapter, what they think of the main characters. Who do they like? Who don't they trust? Why?
● Ask: *If you met the Colonel, would you call him names, as the boys did?* Ask the children to support and explain their opinions with textual evidence.
● Discuss what the author intended when he created the characters. Ask: *How does he influence readers to share his viewpoint?* Encourage the children to look for style of speech – is it formal or informal? Note body language and actions – for example, at the funeral: *his hand clutching the lapel of his jacket.*
● Talk about the Colonel's power and influence over the community – he is the owner of many homes and so forth.
● Invite the children to write a paragraph or two describing the Colonel's character. Ask them to support their opinions of him using textual evidence and explain how the author uses language and direct speech (often formal, aloof).

> **Differentiation**
> **For older/more confident learners:** Challenge these children to continue a diary of observations about the Colonel. Ask: *How was he able to influence Molly's parents? Why did he want to?*
> **For younger/less confident learners:** Hand out copies of photocopiable page 15 to help these children to organise their thoughts before writing.

Plot, character and setting

Right and wrong

> **Objective:** To understand underlying themes, causes and points of view.
> **What you need:** Copies of *Private Peaceful*.
> **Cross-curricular link:** PSHE.

What to do

● Ask the children to list things the boys did wrong, including blowing raspberries, name-calling, feeding Big Joe rabbit droppings and fighting in the playground.
● Discuss which are naughty or unkind. Are any justified or understandable? Ask: *How do Tommo and Charlie feel about each 'crime' when they are discovered?*
● Talk about Tommo's feelings of guilt over Father's death, his personal blame that he didn't run and that if he had, his father would be alive. Ask: *Who is to blame?*
● Look together at how Mother deals with her sons' misbehaviour. Ask: *Is she is 'fair' to them?*

How does their feeding Big Joe rabbit droppings differ from their other pranks? (Unwarranted, cold-blooded cruelty.)
● Ask: *When the Colonel blackmails Mother to work for him, why does Tommo 'almost' tell Charlie his secret then?* (He feels responsible for the consequences of his father's death.) *If Tommo had told his brother what happened, would Charlie have blamed or reassured him?* Encourage the children to justify their opinions.

> **Differentiation**
> **For older/more confident learners:** Ask these children to write about a misdeed (real or imagined) that they think is justifiable, and a misdeed that they think wrong under any circumstances. Encourage them to explain the reasons for their decisions.
> **For younger/less confident learners:** Make a class list of the brothers' wrongdoings in order of seriousness. Ask the children to explain why they think one is worse than another.

Faith and beliefs

> **Objective:** Make notes on and use evidence from across a text to explain events or ideas.
> **What you need:** Copies of *Private Peaceful* and copies of photocopiable page 16.
> **Cross-curricular link:** PSHE.

What to do

● Sort the children into groups of five or six, appointing a scribe to each.
● Provide each scribe with a copy of photocopiable page 16. Ask the children to discuss the nature of religion, superstition, faith and belief, then position the listed words according to their findings.
● As a whole class, share opinions. Compare belief and faith (certainty in mind and heart without proof) and knowledge (measurable evidence). Invite the children to compare spells and incantations with prayer; religious rituals,

such as swinging incense, lighting candles, crossing oneself, with superstitious rituals, such as crossing fingers or making a wish.
● Talk about the *Private Peaceful* characters' responses to religion and superstition. Invite the children to find examples of both, determining which are which and where they overlap (such as placing articles in Father's coffin at his funeral).
● Ask how, when and why Tommo's beliefs change as he grows older.

> **Differentiation**
> **For older/more confident learners:** Ask these children to discuss how singing 'Oranges and Lemons' affects each of the Peaceful boys. Ask: *What makes this different from either religion or superstition? How does it make them feel better?*
> **For younger/less confident learners:** Invite these children to share any superstitions or rituals they perform and to explain why.

Plot, character and setting

Powerful persuasion

> **Objective:** To recognise rhetorical devices used to argue, persuade, mislead and sway the reader.
> **What you need:** Copies of *Private Peaceful*, writing materials, enlarged copy of Extract 2 (page 9) and enlarged copy of photocopiable page 17.

What to do

● When the children have read the chapter entitled 'Twenty-eight minutes past one', display an enlarged copy of Extract 2. Together, annotate the text according to the notes on page 7.
● Invite the children to list metaphorical phrases and write their meaning alongside, such as *no picnic*: neither fun nor relaxing, or *knock the stuffing out of them*: destroy them.
● Circle all the question marks in the speech. Discuss how these questions are rhetorical – not inviting any answer except agreement.

● Underline persuasive, imperative, evocative phrases: *mark my words*, *here on your doorstep*, *brave little* Belgium. Discuss how the sergeant major reinforces his words.
● Display an enlarged copy of the poster on page 17. Ask the children what the sergeant major's rhetoric and the poster's message have in common. Ask: *Why did the soldiers wear red uniforms to march through Hatherleigh that day?*

> **Differentiation**
> **For older/more confident learners:** Ask the children to explain why Tommo found himself joining in with the shouted responses from the crowd.
> **For younger/less confident learners:** Ask these children to explain how the combined effect of seeing Jimmy Parsons stand forward to volunteer, and having an old woman imply he was a coward, influenced Tommo's decision.

A common theme

> **Objective:** To compare how a common theme is presented in poetry, prose and other media.
> **What you need:** Copies of *Private Peaceful*, enlarged copies of page 18 and Extract 3 (page 10).
> **Cross-curricular link:** PSHE.

What to do

● Please note: the first of these extracts explores the horror of war using powerful language and imagery. It is perhaps best suited to children of sufficient emotional maturity to cope.
● Display enlarged copies of Extract 3 (page 10) and the poetry extracts (page 18). Explain that the poems arose from direct observation; the novel was written around 90 years later.
● Explain that the Latin title *Dulce et decorum est...*, (It is a sweet and right thing...) is completed in the final line of the full poem with 'the old lie' *...pro patria mori* (...to die for your country).
● Read both extracts aloud to the class.
● Invite the children to compare the poetic

and prose descriptions of gas attacks. Underline similar phrases: the repeated cry of *Gas!*; *we fumble clumsily, feverishly...* and *an ecstasy of fumbling*; *deadly tendrils... long yellow wisps* and *misty panes and thick green light*; *coughing, retching, choking* and *guttering, choking, drowning*. Ask why Owen chose the word *ecstasy*. (The thrill of relief.)
● Determine together how far Owen's poem may have influenced the author. Ask: *How is each text effective for its purpose?*
● Compare Binyon's verses, with their focus on pride and honour rather than horror. Discuss which poem would comfort grieving relatives, and why.

> **Differentiation**
> **For older/more confident learners:** Ask the children to discuss how far Tommo would agree that *Dulce et decorum est pro patria mori* is, indeed, an old lie.
> **For younger/less confident learners:** Invite these children to search out more poems by Wilfred Owen and other war poets, such as Siegfried Sassoon.

Plot, character and setting

Reading between the lines

> **Objective:** To read between the lines and find evidence for their interpretation.
> **What you need:** Copies of *Private Peaceful* and writing materials.

What to do

● Ask the children to read the two letters that Charlie receives. Draw attention to Tommo's comment: *Everyone I love is in them.*
● Explain that when you read a text, you can take the words 'at face value'. Then you can look deeper at how to interpret what is said (and what is *not* said), to infer the writer's real feelings and situation, awareness or ignorance, or hidden meaning. This is called 'reading between the lines'.
● Invite the children to re-read the letters, attempting to read between the lines.

● Ask questions to help the children's thinking. What does this tell us about Mother's awareness of life at the battlefront? *He looks thinner... I do not think he has been eating enough and have told him to do so in future.* Ask the children how this informs the reader about the toll the war has taken on Charlie. Why does Charlie address Tommo as 'Private Peaceful'?
● As a class, discuss the family's characters and responses to their current situation.

> **Differentiation**
> **For older/more confident learners:** Invite these children to write a few paragraphs on how the letters inform the reader and reveal characteristics of the main characters.
> **For younger/less confident learners:** Ask an adult to work with these children, to read together and point out lines that have hidden depths for discussion.

Behaving in character

> **Objective:** To compare the usefulness of techniques such as visualisation, prediction and empathy in exploring the meaning of texts.
> **What you need:** Copies of *Private Peaceful* and writing materials.
> **Cross-curricular link:** PSHE.

What to do

● Ask each child to think of a family member or close friend. They should spend five minutes with a partner asking and answering questions about their chosen person's behaviour, such as: *What would they do if you were home late? Would they share their sweets? Would they like to go bungee jumping?*
● Explain that, in stories, as in real life, people's behaviour is largely predictable. So unusual behaviour will make us say, 'It's not like him.'
● Ask how well the children can visualise each character in *Private Peaceful*. Ask: *Do the characters behave 'in character'?*

● Explain that the children are to be literacy detectives. Their task is to look back through the book and work out how and where the author feeds information about his characters and how their minds work.
● Begin the investigation with Big Joe. List these adjectives that describe the character about whom Tommo says *our lives all revolved*: *happy, gentle, kind, generous, friendly, forgiving, trusting, innocent.* Ask the children to retrieve, note and discuss examples of behaviour, events, description or direct speech that support each of these descriptions of Big Joe.

> **Differentiation**
> **For older/more confident learners:** Challenge these children to act as detectives and investigate another leading character, collecting textual evidence.
> **For younger/less confident learners:** Help these children to create a fact file about Big Joe, to include what makes him happy, how he is kind to others, his family members and what he likes about them.

Plot, character and setting

Character clues

● What do these quotations reveal about the Colonel's character and beliefs? How far, if at all, and when, is the Colonel being sincere?

Quotation	Notes and observations
He declares that James Peaceful was a good man, one of the best workers... the salt of the earth, always cheerful... never once late for work.	
"I'll teach you, you young ruffians!" he roared. "I'll teach you."	
"It may seem a little indelicate to broach the subject so soon after your late husband's sad and untimely death," the Colonel was saying. He wasn't looking at Mother.	
"…as for the other one, there is the lunatic asylum in Exeter. I'm sure a place could be found for – "	
"I shall need your agreement within the week… And once again my condolences."	

● What do you think is the author's opinion of the Colonel? How does he make the reader share his opinion?

_____

_____

_____

_____

Faith and beliefs

● Copy words from the table below to where they belong.
  ● Some apply to **religious belief**.
  ● Some apply to **superstitious belief**.
  ● Some belong to **both**. (Write these where the boxes overlap.)
  ● Some belong to **neither** box. (Write these in the box at the bottom.)

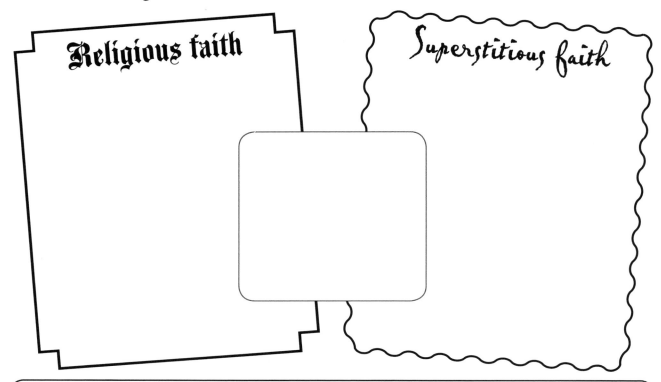

Religious faith

Superstitious faith

Belief in neither God and Heaven nor superstitions:

hope	sacrifice	faith	ritual
spells or incantations	luck	Bible	knowledge
supernatural power	prayer	God	magic

Powerful persuasion

● Lord Kitchener (1850–1916) appears on this famous recruitment campaign poster. He was Secretary of State for War during the early war years.

Photograph © Mary Evans Picture Library 2008.

A common theme

- This is an extract from *Dulce et Decorum Est* by Wilfred Owen (1893–1918), a poet who experienced the trenches first-hand.

> *Gas! GAS! Quick, boys! - An ecstasy of fumbling*
> *Fitting the clumsy helmets just in time,*
> *But someone still was yelling out and stumbling*
> *And flound'ring like a man in fire or lime...*
> *Dim through the misty panes and thick green light*
> *As under a green sea, I saw him drowning.*
> *In all my dreams before my helpless sight*
> *He plunges at me, guttering, choking, drowning.*
>
> Wilfred Owen

- This is an extract from For the Fallen by Laurence Binyon (1869–1943) an English poet, dramatist, and art scholar.

- The second of the following verses is often read at memorials, and services of thanksgiving, in honour of soldiers who died in battle.

> *They went with songs to battle, they were young,*
> *Straight of limb, true of eye, steady and aglow.*
> *They were staunch to the end against odds uncounted;*
> *They fell with their faces to the foe.*
>
> *They shall not grow old, as we that are left grow old:*
> *Age shall not weary them, nor the years condemn.*
> *At the going down of the sun and in the morning*
> *We will remember them.*
>
> © 1914, Laurence Binyon

Talk about it

Interpretations

> **Objective:** To reflect on how working in role helps to explore complex issues.
> **What you need:** Copies of *Private Peaceful*, individual copies of photocopiable page 22 and writing materials.
> **Cross-curricular link:** PSHE.

What to do

● Hand out copies of page 22 for reference as children read the chapter entitled 'Fourteen minutes past two'.

● List the recruits that Tommo knows, with their former occupations. Ask: *How well has their work prepared them for warfare?*

● Explain that life expectancy in the trenches was measured in days.

● Discuss how important it is for soldiers to obey orders unquestioningly, to survive. Divide the class into groups and ask each to list which events in this chapter help them prepare for action, and which become bullying.

● Share the findings. Point out how the corporals explain why to dig deep: a major survival factor.

● Charlie has stood up to bullies before. Ask: *How wise it is for him to stand up to Hanley? Which metaphor indicates how Charlie's stand affects other recruits?* (*Charlie was swiping at the wasp... stinging all of us.*)

> **Differentiation**
> **For older/more confident learners:** Ask these children to practise a fire drill for evacuating the classroom in an orderly way. Ask one child to act being uncooperative and invite the group to improvise possible consequences of this behaviour.
> **For younger/less confident learners:** In a large space, invite the children to run with their school bags above their heads, and time how long they can do it before their arms begin to ache.

Changing times

> **Objective:** To use the techniques of dialogical talk to explore ideas, topics or issues.
> **What you need:** Copies of *Private Peaceful*, copies of photocopiable page 23 and writing materials.

What to do

● Invite the children to imagine life after 1918. Ask: *How would the respective mothers of Charlie Peaceful and Jimmy Parsons feel? Which mother could grieve openly and hold her head high? Which mother might feel alienated, knowing that neighbours looked down on her son and his family? Why would he be judged as behaving shamefully?*

● Ask the children: *Were both Jimmy and Charlie brave? How much did Charlie's behaviour contribute to his death, and how much Sergeant Hanley's personal vendetta?*

● Ask the children if they think it was wise of Charlie to disobey the sergeant's order. Point out that if Charlie had obeyed orders, he would probably have died anyway, but 'honourably', from enemy fire.

● Explain to the class that actions from historical times were based on accepted behaviour in that era. Ask: *Is it right or wrong to pardon them now? Is it too late?*

● Read the postscript written in 2003. Explain that in 2006 the British Government did grant a posthumous pardon to all British soldiers executed by their own army in the First World War.

> **Differentiation**
> **For older/more confident learners:** Encourage the children to research this subject further and look for articles about real-life Private Harry Farr, whose family fought for 90 years to clear his name. Hold a debate on the pros and cons of posthumous pardons.
> **For younger/less confident learners:** Give children copies of page 23 to read, discuss and evaluate. Can they decide on and justify their own opinions?

Talk about it

Motif and movies

> **Objective:** To understand different ways to take the lead and support others in a group.
> **What you need:** Copies of *Private Peaceful*, writing and art materials.
> **Cross-curricular links:** Music, drama, ICT.

What to do

● Invite suggestions of recurring themes and images in *Private Peaceful*, especially any that appear in both past and present sections, such as the mouse and the singing of 'Oranges and Lemons'. Explain that such a repeated element is called a motif (or 'leitmotif').

● Talk about the motifs' significance: the connotations of 'Oranges and Lemons' (the last two lines are thought to refer to public executions and the younger brothers use it as a song of resistance against authority figures) and the robust ubiquity of the innocent mouse.

● Arrange the children in groups, appointing roles: leader, scribe, mentor, reporter and text researchers. Ask them to imagine planning a film of the book. Encourage discussion of how to use these motifs, visually or aurally, in title sequence or credits. Ask: *How might the camera operator or sound technician alert viewers to their recurrence?*

● Ask reporters to share their group's suggestions with the class. Discuss how effectively audio-visual techniques can present the written word.

> **Differentiation**
> **For older/more confident learners:** Invite the children to cast familiar actors from film or TV in different roles.
> **For younger/less confident learners:** Provide page references to help these children to locate incidents involving the mouse or song motifs. Ask them to design a flyer advertising the film of the book, using one or more motifs.

Power and control

> **Objective:** To identify and report the main points emerging from discussion.
> **What you need:** Copies of *Private Peaceful*, copies of photocopiable page 24 and writing materials.
> **Cross-curricular link:** PSHE.

What to do

● Ask the children if they can recall Charlie's reaction when Tommo returns from the recruitment campaign in Hatherleigh. Remind them that he says: *I'll shoot a rat because it might bite me. I'll shoot a rabbit because I can eat it. Why would I ever want to shoot a German? Never even met a German.*

● Discuss and compare the logic behind Charlie's reasoning, and the cold-blooded vindictiveness of the Colonel's shooting Bertha. Can the children answer Molly's rhetorical question *Why?* (Revenge for the raspberry-blowing incident? For poaching? To demonstrate power? To punish Charlie?) Ask: *How is Bertha useful to Big Joe?*

● Talk about how the Colonel (as well as the head teacher, and the army officers) represents authority and how Charlie is unusual in openly challenging him.

● Hand out copies of photocopiable page 24 for the children to read and respond to in groups, with reference to the book.

● Share responses with the whole class. Ask: *Is true respect won through power and control, or is it earned by behaviour and attitudes?*

> **Differentiation**
> **For older/more confident learners:** Ask the children to compare how differently Sergeant Hanley and Captain Wilkes treat the soldiers and how the soldiers respond.
> **For younger/less confident learners:** Have an adult oversee a group discussion, helping these children to locate textual evidence to support their opinions.

Talk about it

Dramatic dialogue

Objective: To perform a scripted scene making use of dramatic convention.
What you need: Copies of *Private Peaceful*, writing materials, whiteboard and pens.
Cross-curricular link: Drama.

What to do

● You may wish to spend two sessions on this activity (one for preparation and one for performance).
● Re-read the episode in the chapter entitled 'Twenty to eleven', from when the Colonel knocks the door, to where the whole family is singing.
● Ask the children to imagine developing this episode into a script for performance. List potential stage directions for characters, as suggested by the class.
● Demonstrate how to simplify the phrasing and use the present tense, so *She took her time... before*

she opened the door will become, say, *slowly, calmly smoothes apron and hair before opening door.*
● Discuss how the stage directions communicate a character's personality, mood, preoccupations and priorities, enhancing the spoken word.
● Working in pairs, ask the children to create a script for the Colonel and Mother, with convenential layout (including bracketed stage instructions).
● Invite the children to perform the scene in character, attempting to convey the underlying feelings or objectives alongside the spoken text.

Differentiation
For older/more confident learners: Challenge these children to learn their parts by heart.
For younger/less confident learners: Use sticky notes in different colours to highlight respective dialogue and help the children to locate the stage directions correctly.

Highlighting history

Objective: To tailor the structure, vocabulary and delivery of a talk or presentation so that it is helpfully sequenced and supported by gesture or other visual aids as appropriate.
What you need: Copies of *Private Peaceful*, enlarged copy of Extract 3 (page 10), copies of photocopiable page 22, First World War memorabilia and artefacts (if available), history books and internet access.
Cross-curricular link: History.

What to do

● Display Extract 3 and read it aloud. Ask the children to list the names of any equipment that the soldiers use: gas masks, rifles with detachable bayonets, helmets.
● Although what they are reading is an extract from a historical novel that is fiction, ask the children: *How many things on your lists are factually accurate in relation to life in the trenches during the First World War (1914–1918)?*
● Invite the children to return to the book, and

find further factual aspects that describe the front line. Point out that these facts can be turned into a non-fiction account of life in the trenches. Remind them to use the glossary provided on photocopiable page 22. Encourage them to use books and the internet and add their sources of information to their notes. Make available any suitable artefacts for the children to examine.
● Invite the children to prepare a five-minute talk, using quotations or recording, on 'Life in the Trenches in the First World War'.

Differentiation
For older/more confident learners: Challenge the children to tailor their speech for another class or their parents. Can they interview a relative about their father's or grandfather's wartime experience?
For younger/less confident learners: Let these children work in pairs. Guide them in how to sequence their presentation. Suggest using numbered cards with bullet points.

READ & RESPOND: Activities based on Private Peaceful

Interpretations

Glossary of terms relating to the First World War (1914–1918)

Court martial – trial of a soldier for breaking military law, for misdeeds such as disobeying orders, deserting, falling asleep on duty

Dug out – a protective hole cut out to one side of a trench, used for sleeping or eating

Fire step – step cut into the wall of a trench from which a soldier can peer over the parapet and see no-man's-land and the enemy trench line beyond

Fixed bayonet – short sword attached to the barrel of a rifle

Fritz – name to represent any German soldier

Hun – insulting term for Germans

King's shilling (taking the...) – a shilling once being a soldier's daily pay, a term used to describe enlisting in the army

No-man's-land – area of barren land between British and German lines of trenches

Padre – army chaplain

Stand to – a pre-dawn and dusk half-hour or hour-long watch (times when enemy attack was most likely) when a soldier stood on the fire step with loaded rifle and fixed bayonet

Tommy – name to represent any British soldier

Trench – a dug-out area in the ground where soldiers could live and walk along, while keeping their heads below enemy fire level

Trench foot – a foot infection caused by cold, wet, insanitary conditions, as in the trenches

Whizzbang – a bomb shell that made a whizzing sound followed by an explosion

Wipers – English pronunciation of Ypres, in Flanders, Belgium (normally pronounced *eep-rr*)

Illustration © 2010, Karen Donnelly.

Talk about it

SECTION 5

Changing times

● Three years after *Private Peaceful* was first published, the British Government granted a posthumous pardon to all British First World War soldiers shot for cowardice or desertion.

● Almost a century after the war, there is still disagreement about pardoning all soldiers, without knowing the precise details of each individual set of circumstances.

● Read the views below. Discuss them with your group. Write a paragraph, explaining whether you think it was right or wrong to grant such a pardon. Talk about why you think it didn't happen sooner.

1917: "My brother Harry had been gassed. He was suffering from shell shock. He needed medical help, not a vile, shameful, death."

1918: "As his sergeant, I had to report Private Brown. If I had shown compassion, and let him off, then others would have disobeyed orders, too. We would have lost the war if the Hun saw our men running scared."

1950: "Three of my uncles' names are on the war memorial. They all died in action in Ypres. Only one of their bodies was ever found. Cowards don't deserve to have their names inscribed alongside comrades they abandoned."

1965: "My grandfather's name is missing off the war memorial in our village. He was a boy of 15 – too young to enlist – and fought bravely. Exhausted, he fell asleep on watch. At his 20-minute trial he had no one to present his case."

2006: "When my great-great-grandfather refused to go over the top, he was found guilty of cowardice and shot at dawn. In fact he was suffering from shell shock. Our family is now free of the stigma and shame."

2003: "People like Charlie thought they knew better than their superiors. Army orders have to be obeyed by ALL soldiers; not just some. They deserved their punishment."

Talk about it

Power and control

● In their different ways, at different levels, both the Colonel and Charlie have control or influence over other people in their family and community. List any of these titles that could be used to describe them.

landlord	poacher	rebel
employer	magistrate	farmhand

Colonel

_____

_____

_____

_____

Charlie

_____

_____

_____

_____

● Now read these statements:
  ● The Colonel provides homes and employment, and implements the law.
  ● When the Colonel overhears the Peaceful boys blowing raspberries, he threatens, "I'll teach you."
  ● When the Colonel insists that Charlie enlist in the army, he uses blackmail, threatening to make Charlie's family homeless, breaking a promise to his wife.
  ● Charlie poaches (steals!) from the Colonel, to feed his hungry family.
  ● When the Colonel advises Molly's parents to keep her away from the Peaceful family, Charlie and Molly defy her parents.

● Discuss (and make notes on the back of this sheet): Which, of Charlie or the Colonel, do you consider the better role model? Explain your answer.

Illustration © 2010, Karen Donnelly.

Get writing

Engage and entertain

> **Objective:** To use different narrative techniques to engage and entertain the reader.
> **What you need:** Copies of *Private Peaceful*, enlarged copy of Extract 1 (page 8) and writing materials.

What to do

● Display Extract 1 and take turns to read it aloud. Talk about the present tense, and first person. Ask: *What effect does this have?* (Sounds as if it's happening now; involves the reader who identifies with the narrator.)
● Point out that many of the shorter sentences contain fewer than ten words. Discuss the effect of such short sentences in between longer ones. Ask: *How else does the author emphasise the nervous breathiness of how young Tommo is feeling?* Alert the children to the connectives in the longer sentences: *and, but* and *because*.
● Lead a discussion of the content (see the notes on page 7), drawing attention to the direct speech and what it conveys about the boys' relationship and Charlie's knowledge of Tommo.
● Invite the children to tell a partner about their first day at school. Advise them to ask each other questions, such as: *How did friends and family prepare you? Were you excited or anxious?*
● Ask the children to write a few paragraphs, in the present tense, first person, describing their first day. They should try to create atmosphere and include detail. Encourage them to begin with an intriguing line and find an angle that will entertain their reader.

> **Differentiation**
> **For older/more confident learners:** Encourage the children to check through their writing and edit it.
> **For younger/less confident learners:** Ask these children to make notes planning the main content of each paragraph before beginning to write.

Picturesque persuasion

> **Objective:** To choose and combine words, images and other features for particular effects.
> **What you need:** Copies of *Private Peaceful*, enlarged copy of Extract 2 (page 9), copies of photocopiable page 28 and writing materials.
> **Cross-curricular link:** Drama.

What to do

● Display Extract 2 and highlight the metaphorical phrases (*beat about the bush, no picnic, here on your doorstep, taken a fair slice, beat them at their own game, gobble us up, knock the stuffing out of them*). Encourage the children to infer their meanings.
● Discuss why the sergeant major uses these phrases. Ask: *What is he trying to achieve?* (To increase impact, shock, fear, urgency and moral pressure through vivid imagery.)
● Talk about Tommo's thoughts when Jimmy Parsons steps forward, when the old woman challenges him, and as he leaves. Compare how Charlie must have felt when blackmailed by the Colonel.
● Hand out copies of photocopiable page 28 for the children to read, sort and translate the figurative expressions.
● Invite the children to write a paragraph along similar lines to that in Extract 2 but with Mother as the speaker, trying to dissuade her sons from enlisting.

> **Differentiation**
> **For older/more confident learners:** Ask two children to role-play Charlie and Tommo while two others play Mother and the sergeant major, using powerful metaphors within their persuasive speeches.
> **For younger/less confident learners:** Invite the children to sort the phrases into two piles of persuasion, for and against joining the army. Help them to use these phrases to create Mother's imaginary speech.

Get writing

Now and then

Objective: To experiment with different narrative forms and styles to write their own stories.
What you need: Copies of *Private Peaceful*, copies of photocopiable page 29 and writing materials.

What to do

● Ask: *From whose viewpoint are we looking throughout the narrative?* (Tommo's.) Argue that, even though it is the one character's perspective, readers are looking from two viewpoints – as Tommo, the child; and as Tommo, the reflective adult.
● Find examples of where the present and reflective sections of chapters clearly link, as if sparking a train of thought, such as eating (second chapter) and mice (third chapter).
● List some common experiences that children will have had, such as buying new shoes or celebrating a birthday.
● Invite individuals to recount an episode from their infancy, such as falling off a bike.
● Ask the children to discuss the impact of experience, changing needs, values, expectations and lack of innocence on such occasions now that they are older.
● Hand out copies of photocopiable page 29 to help the children to plan a piece of biographical writing in the style of Michael Morpurgo's fictional writing in *Private Peaceful*.

Differentiation
For older/more confident learners: Challenge the children to extend their accounts into a fictional story based on their changing experience.
For younger/less confident learners: Use a voice-recorder as children tell their anecdotes. Guide the children as they transcribe their accounts.

Dear Tommo

Objective: In non-narrative, to establish, balance and maintain viewpoints.
What you need: Copies of *Private Peaceful* and writing materials.

What to do

● Ask the children to re-read the letters that Tommo receives in 'Nearly Four o'Clock'. Discuss why Charlie told his mother they were having *a fine time* in Belgium. (To protect and encourage her? To lessen her concern?) Invite them to compare what he writes to his brother: *I'd rather not tell anyone* (where they've been and what they've been doing).
● Discuss how, during a crisis, people may be sparing with the truth. Ask: *How and why might they be more honest after the crisis is over?* (The worst is over, the end known; no uncertainty.)
● Remind the children of Molly's claim that she has told baby Tommo all about his *brave uncle*. Ask: *Why, when a newborn won't understand?*
(To show Tommo how much she loves and thinks of him.)
● As the children read on and learn the fate of Charlie, invite them to write a letter from Charlie to his baby son, for young Tommo to read when he is grown up. Encourage them to explain how and why he acted as he did. They must think about what he will say about his brother and Molly and young Tommo's grandparents. Ask: *How much will he write of the war, and how much of his home life?* Remind the children how Charlie says they are *two separate worlds*.

Differentiation
For older/more confident learners: Challenge the children to imagine the young Tommo reading their letter, and write an imaginary reply to the father he never knew. Encourage them to research the period.
For younger/less confident learners: Give these children suggestions of how to begin their letter, such as: *My dear son, By the time you read this you will already know a little about me, your father.*

Get writing

Reviews

Objective: To write and present a text independently with readers and purpose in mind.
What you need: Copies of *Private Peaceful* and writing materials.

What to do

• Establish through consensus, the purpose of a book review. Ask: *What would you want to learn from reading a review? How much storyline should it reveal? How would it encourage or deter you from choosing to read the book?* Advise the children to read the back cover blurb and observe how it does not give away too much of the plot.

• Write on the board the quotations from newspaper reviews that appear on the back cover: *…a deeply moving portrayal of camaraderie and courage, innocence and brutality – Daily Telegraph; Written from the heart – Observer; A poignant, elegiac novel – Daily Mail.*

• Talk about why the cover designers chose these particular words: how do they help inform the reader and sell the book? (Define *elegiac*: like an elegy: a mournful song in sorrow for the dead.)

• Hold a class discussion on the question: *How and why does the book succeed as a tribute to those who were executed by their own country?*

• Ask the children to plan and write their own review of the book. They must decide first whether to aim their review at adults or their peers.

Differentiation
For older/more confident learners: Invite these children to present their reviews aurally to the rest of the group, allowing the listeners to ask questions.
For younger/less confident learners: Ask the children to choose from their own review a suitable quotation that might be used by the book's publishers to promote the book.

Words in action

Objective: To reflect independently and critically on their writing, to edit and improve it.
What you need: Copies of *Private Peaceful*, writing materials, enlarged copy of Extract 3 (page 10), copies of photocopiable page 30 and a thesaurus.

What to do

• Read Extract 3 together. Ask the children to define feelings in the passage, such as fear, panic, urgency and sharpened senses.

• Ask: *How does the author convey the burst of energy that the men suddenly have?* Highlight graphic adverbs and verbs, such as *feverishly, yelling, frantically* and *grab*. Explain how the brain produces adrenalin, which flows round the body, helping it to react faster.

• Point out how young readers cannot share such an experience, but through strong descriptive language, and direct speech, they can begin to empathise with the characters.

• Ask the children to share with a partner a moment when they have had to act quickly, playing sport or trying to avoid an accident.

• Explain that in any emergency, large or small, time seems to slow down. Many thoughts can go through a person's mind and they can perform a number of successive actions in, apparently, hardly any time at all.

• Challenge the children to write a passage based on a real or imagined experience. Let them use photocopiable page 30 to help their planning.

Differentiation
For older/more confident learners: Ask the children to read their passage aloud to themselves, making sure they vary their words, or make simple verbs more dramatic.
For younger/less confident learners: Listen to these children telling their story and point out ways in which they can embellish it to prolong the action and add detail, especially drawing on the five senses.

Picturesque persuasion

● Read and sort these figurative expressions. Tick them in **red** if the sergeant major uses them, **or might do so.** Tick them in **green** if Mother might use them forcefully.

● Rephrase each expression in your own words to show what they mean.

Shall we knock the stuffing out of them? Shall we beat them into submission?
Are you tied to your mother's apron strings?
What if you kick the bucket?
He's no man who cannot say 'no'.
Who will take the King's shilling?
The game is not worth the candle.
You'll be like a fish out of water.
Look before you leap.
Put your hand to the plough.
If we don't stop them they'll be right here on your doorstep.

Now and then

● Choose one of the events below or invent your own. Think of your motivations, reasons and interests in each case, and add notes related to your experiences. Use your notes to draft a first-person account in two sections.

Recent event:	Past event:
Buying shoes ● Reason: going to a disco or party ● Not like school shoes, must be fashionable, must match clothes _____ _____	*Buying shoes* ● *Reason: grown out of old ones* ● *Must be flat and waterproof, brown or black, with extra toe-room for growth* _____ _____
Celebrating my birthday _____ _____ _____ _____	*Celebrating my birthday* _____ _____ _____ _____

● Before writing think about how to:
  ● Write the recent event as if it is happening now.
  ● Write the past event as a memory.
  ● Change tenses or keep both sections in the present.
  ● Involve your senses: sight, sound, touch, taste, smell.
  ● Talk about what you are thinking, your feelings, hopes and fears.

Get writing

Words in action

● Describe in simple terms a real or imaginary situation that demands your instant action. You may exaggerate a real situation to add excitement.

[ ]

● List some verbs you might use to describe the event. Use a thesaurus to add to the drama of the scene. For example, instead of *get*, use *grab, haul, heave, drag, shift* or *catch*.

[ ]

● Add a list of adverbs, such as *frantically*, to boost your verbs. (Do not use too many!)

[ ]

● Now draft your descriptive narrative on the back of this sheet.

Illustration © 2010, Karen Donnelly.

Assessment

Assessment advice

Although the syntax of the narrative makes this an easy read, children may need help with dated terms and concepts, and with the structure of the novel, as it switches between present and past in time and tense. Check that they recognise the separation function of the butterfly symbol.

There is much to be gleaned from the novel, not only about the First World War, but also about the whole period, the social hierarchy, lifestyle, expectations, and treatment of people with brain damage, for example. Questioning the children during the reading will reveal how far they are able to 'read between the lines' and discern deeper implications of superficial statements, and the significance of lines such as *There was no money in the mug on the mantelpiece*: the ultimate financial reserves.

You can explore such issues as the forelock-tugging subservience that Charlie resisted, the nature of cowardice and bravery, bullying, love and loyalty, honesty and dishonesty. Observe how far the children's own experiences inform their reading of this book. Ask them to recognise and explain the 'grey areas' of what is right and wrong. We often say, 'It's not fair!' Ask: *How far can life ever be completely just?*

A sharp learning curve

> **Assessment focus:** To read between the lines and find evidence for their interpretation.
> **What you need:** Copies of *Private Peaceful*, copies of photocopiable page 32 and writing materials.
> **Cross-curricular link:** PSHE.

What to do
● Talk briefly about each of the elements quoted on photocopiable page 32 (innocence, love, courage and cowardice).
● Point out that the boys' journey from infancy to adulthood, and from rural life to wartime soldier, required what today we would call a 'sharp learning curve'. That is, they needed to adapt to a different culture, unfamiliar routines and hostility quickly and efficiently. It is also a journey from innocence to experience, which those who stayed at home would never fully know.
● Point out how many different kinds of love there are in the book – brotherly, friendly, parental and romantic, as well as love of places and nature.
● Briefly discuss with the children the nature of cowardice and courage. Invite them to compare how Jimmy Parson's childish nature came to be channelled into his soldiering, while 'Horrible' Hanley's soldiering gave him power to formalise his cowardly bullying – effectively with approval of higher office, and safely immune from vengeance.
● Clarify that bravery is acting despite fear and that, as the saying goes, 'anyone who says they are never afraid is either a fool or a liar'. Point out that feelings of cowardice are mentioned but overcome.
● Hand out copies of photocopiable page 32 along with copies of *Private Peaceful*. Ask the children to complete the questions on the sheet, finding quotations from the text to support their opinions.

A sharp learning curve

Michael Morpurgo's novel *Private Peaceful* explores 'innocence and love, courage and cowardice'.

● Find a quotation from the book to support each of these four aspects.
● Explain how the quotation demonstrates these elements.

Innocence
(page   ) _____

Love
(page   ) _____

Courage
(page   ) _____

Cowardice
(page   ) _____